Buying a Franchise – Is it Right for Me?

A Handbook for

Avoiding the Top 10 Mistakes People Make When Researching Franchises

"Special Bonus Chapter for Military Veterans"

By Lonnie Helgerson, CFE

Copyright © 2011 by Lonnie D. Helgerson and Helgerson Franchise Group. All rights reserved.

Published by Helgerson Franchise Group

www.HelgersonFranchiseGroup.com

The Library of Congress has catalogued this paperback edition as follows:

First Edition

Buying a Franchise - Is it Right for Me?

ISBN 978-0-615-54322-2

Printed in the United States of America.

Acknowledgments

Special thanks go to my loving wife Linette and our good friends David & Jessica Tolson for their tremendous assistance on this project.

This book is dedicated to all of the hard-working small business franchise owners that get up every morning and keep America rolling with your goods and services!

Table of Contents

Introduction

Congratulations - we have both succeeded so far! For you, reading this handbook means that you are contemplating the world of franchise ownership and have taken your first steps towards that goal. As for me, I have managed to catch your attention long enough to offer up some straight-forward advice on your franchise quest.

You won't find a lot of fluff or hype about the successes of franchising in this handbook. What you will find are 10 mistakes or assumptions that people have sometimes made while investigating or contemplating a franchised business. My goal with this book is to help you avoid buying a franchise at all - if franchising is not suited for you.

Franchising is definitely not for everyone, but there are hundreds of thousands of people who enjoy running their own business and the lifestyle that it offers.

As CEO and founder with nearly 30 years of franchise experience, I have witnessed great people enter into a franchise for all the wrong reasons, and in the end it has cost them dearly. On the flip side, I have seen great people enter into a franchise and have ended up being successful beyond their dreams. The difference between them many times - is whether they should have gotten involved with franchising at all.

By reading this handbook I hope that you will find enough information to determine if franchised business ownership is right for you and your goals. Good luck!

The Top 10 Mistakes List

- **Being an Entrepreneur vs. Frantrepreneur**
  - *Franchise systems don't want their wheel reinvented; they want people who can make the wheel turn faster.*
- **Confusing a franchise with a job**
  - *If you only want to work 8-5, don't apply for a franchise.*
- **Assuming you can just try it out awhile**
  - *Franchise Agreements typically average 10 years in length, so be prepared for a long-term business.*
- **Not being financially prepared for the investment**
  - *Starting a business takes cold hard cash - be ready for that.*
- **Working in the business – Not on it**
  - *Franchise systems want business builders - not business workers.*
- **Going it alone**
  - *You will be doomed for failure if your spouse or partner does not support your business interests.*
- **Sticking to what you know**
  - *What you're good at doing today, may not be the best franchise for you.*
- **Having lone wolf syndrome**
  - *Franchising is about consistency and teamwork – you will need to get along with others.*
- **Not sharing your information**
  - *Be prepared to share personal information with a franchise company.*
- **Expecting automatic success**
  - *Franchise systems provide you the tools – you still need to use them and build a business.*

Chapter 1

Being an Entrepreneur vs. Frantrepreneur

Franchising Facts:

- Buying a franchise will put you light years ahead in terms of startup and development time.
- Franchising provides you the support to help you reach your business goals.
- Buying a franchise will provide you training that would take years of experience to acquire.
- Regardless of how good you are at what you do - you have never owned and operated the type of franchise you are evaluating.
- When you decide to sell your business, a franchise brand has more value than "Fred's Sub Sandwiches".

Buying a franchise will put you light years ahead in terms of startup and development time.

Let's face it... running a business can be one of the hardest things you will ever do in your life. But before you even get to the "running" part of your business, you must decide which one is the best fit for you and then get the doors open. There are literally hundreds of details that need to be taken care of before you even open for business. But here are just a few to think about:

- Your Business Plan
- Financing Your Business
- Marketing Your Business
- Real Estate Selection
- Lease Negotiation

- Build out (floor plan, architect, contractors, utilities, permits, etc.)
- Employees (hiring, manuals, etc.)
- Signage (permits, etc.)
- Initial Inventory
- Grand Opening
- Computer & Phone Systems, Point of Sale, etc.
- Employee Training
- Operations Manual
- Accounting Setup
- And the list goes on and on and on...

So now the question is... Have you ever done ALL of this once? Or even twice? How about twenty five times? Or even a hundred times? Your potential franchisor has and that is a very compelling reason to buy one.

Franchise companies have this development thing down to a science. What could take you months or longer on your own, can now be shortened down to weeks, or in some cases days - depending upon which franchise system you join. If you think about this in the right context – compare the savings in time to what you are paying for upfront with your franchise fee.

The quicker you are open for business - the quicker the cash register starts to ring. The extra sales brought in by being open twelve months, six months or even a month sooner (depending upon the franchise concept) could easily exceed the initial franchise fee.

Bottom line... Franchising springboards you into being open and generating sales much faster than doing it on your own.

Franchising provides you the support to help you reach your business goals.

OK, let me paint a picture for you... When you are a non-franchised independent business - you are literally on your own. No one is there to support or care about you. When you have questions or run into problems with your business; who will you turn to? Your banker?? He will ask you what you are going to do to fix it, not offer suggestions on how. Then he will put you on a watch list because he is nervous that you are going to default on your business loan. Not a good picture is it?

Franchise companies are not in the business of opening new locations just to watch them go down the tubes - as closed locations do not bode well in trying to grow a national brand. Good franchise companies will want to work in a proactive way with you to try and keep you from getting into trouble. As long as you are willing to work with them - they will coach you along the path of business growth.

If you get into trouble; most franchise companies will work as hard as they can to help you make changes to bring stability back to your business. Remember, it is their brand on the sign and they do not want it to go dark either. Franchisees that listen and work with their franchisor can typically expect to have a viable business much longer than their counterparts that took the route of a non-franchised independent business.

Buying a franchise will provide you training that would take years of experience to acquire.

Again, franchisors have dealt with business problems hundreds, perhaps thousands of times. Their training curriculum reflects that experience. More often than not, you will be trained by a number of executives, staff members operating in specialized areas, or even franchisees in the system. Initial training periods vary depending on the franchise and may include onsite training. Some franchises will even require you to work in an operating unit before you open. You cannot get this kind of training outside of the franchise arena. I do not know of any non-franchised business owner that will train you to go into competition with him!

Business knowledge takes hard knocks to learn… your potential franchisor has been through this. Training is an often overlooked asset that you get when you purchase your franchise. If you had to pay for the combined knowledge that your franchisor has gleaned from their years of hard knocks and their system best practices - believe me it would be a lot more than what you are paying for the franchise fee.

Regardless of how good you are at what you do - you have never owned and operated the type franchise you are evaluating.

This topic is one of my favorites because it involves ego. Let's face it - we all have one whether it is large or small. When buying a franchise, check your ego at the door. Even if you have been in business for years, there are "particulars" and "nuances" about the concept you are looking to buy that only people who have ran one will know.

This is a "business" that you are buying and it involves a great deal of forward vision to keep it going. Let's use computer repair as an example. If you are a great tech and have all of the credentials in the world - does that mean you know how to run a business? Probably not! If you purchase a franchise and get caught up doing the tech work, you never have time to advance the business. In other words, if you work "IN" the business, you can't work "ON" the business.

When evaluating a franchise - open your mind and approach the opportunity in a learning fashion and things will go much smoother for you.

When you decide to sell your business, a franchise brand has more value than "Fred's Sub Sandwiches".

Sorry if your name is Fred - but I have a method to my madness. A national or even a semi-national brand name is typically easier to sell and will bring more value than any independent business. The reason why is generally as a non-franchised independent business, the business itself is so tied to the original owner (sometimes even in name) that often times without the original owner, the business does not make it after the sale.

A franchise has much tighter operations and procedures tied to the brand. As well, new owners go through formalized training to take the existing business to even greater heights. Most franchise companies will assist their owners in selling their business and will advertise it to potential new franchisees looking to enter the system.

Bottom line... SUBWAY® has greater resale value to it than Fred's Sub Sandwiches. Even though it was a Fred that started SUBWAY®...

Success Tips:

- If you're a wheel inventor – franchising is not for you! If you can make their wheel turn faster – you're one step closer.
- When evaluating a franchise concept, ask them about their startup, development and build out assistance. You will find most of them are quite sophisticated.

- Really, really think about the on-going assistance you will receive vs. what you will get on your own. It will add years to the life of your business.
- When attending training; leave your ego at home.
- Try to focus on starting and building a business, not working in one.

Chapter 2

Confusing a franchise with a job

Franchising Facts:

- If you are looking for a job replacement - franchising is <u>NOT</u> for you.
- Yes! Expect to work hard.
- Do not use a franchise for an in-between jobs gig.

If you are looking for a job replacement - franchising is NOT for you.

Yes, we have all heard the stories of someone's Grandpa who worked 18 hours a day, seven days a week building his business and now owns' an island in South Florida. Guess what? They are probably true.

A wise old friend of mine who owned a plumbing business and many investment properties once told me that *"the harder you work, the luckier you get!"* I didn't really understand what he meant until I had owned my businesses for some time. Working hard doesn't necessarily mean physical labor - in this context it means working smarter! For me I work hard because I enjoy what I am doing. After a while, owning a business becomes a lifestyle rather than something you do just to make a living.

Owning a franchise does not mean working normal 8-5 hours, nor does it mean getting paid all the time - at least in the beginning. After you close for the day you must prepare for the next business day, do your accounting, review marketing or advertising, clean up the store, and on, and on. In addition, you can expect some travel for training, regional meetings, yearly convention and so on. When you are building a new business, the bills and business obligations come first - then personal gain. It means paying your employees first even though you might not take a check.

Most people are not ready to make that level of commitment - hence they never own a business. You must be ready to commit yourself that the business comes first *fiscally* and that you will work whatever hours it takes to get it up and running profitably. I always tell people that it could take a year before you start seeing results. A year seems like a long time - but islands are expensive!

Now I am not saying that owning a franchise is all work and no pay, but I am asking you *"Are you willing to commit whatever it takes for the business to make it?"* If not, you might want to stick to your job making someone else rich enough to buy their island.

Yes! Expect to work hard.

Again, I have found working hard, means working smarter. As a business owner, I frequently find myself in the office on a Saturday or Sunday. A strange thing that I love to do is walk around my offices and see which staff members message lights are flashing, if there any faxes lying on the fax machine, etc. It makes me feel good, because it tells me we are in business – doing business. Those little lights flashing mean customers and sales to me, not just more work.

I also love the sound of the telephone ringing!! A ringing telephone is the sound of money, not an interruption of the day. It is all in perspective. I cringe when I hear business owners complain about their phone ringing all day and they cannot get anything done. If that is the case, they are working "in" the business and not "on" the business and they need to make changes.

Another thing that I think about on those weekend office visits is - I bet my competition isn't working today. So that means whatever I do today, puts me that much further ahead of them. Even though you are working longer and harder hours, you realize why you are doing it and the gains made because of it. That is working smarter. Work hard and smart and you too can own an island - hopefully a really expensive one that requires a large yacht to get to!

Do not use a franchise for an in-between jobs gig.

I have heard people tell me that the reason they are looking to buy a franchise is because they cannot find a job. My response to that is "No problem!" as long as the dream job opportunity doesn't come along in the next ten years, because that is the average length of a franchise agreement.

Buying a franchise is serious business – so don't make a mistake of thinking that you will just employ yourself until the next deal comes along. Treat it as a long-term investment that needs to be nurtured and cared for and you will do fine. Wealth does not happen overnight, it is grown from seeds planted years before.

Success Tips:

- Make a commitment that this is a business and not a job.
- Expect to work hard and long days on the business, not in it. (smarter)
- Be patient - it takes time to build a successful business.

Chapter 3

Assuming you can just try it out for awhile

Franchising Facts:

- A franchise agreement is a contractual obligation.
- Don't just hire any lawyer - hire a <u>franchise lawyer</u>.

A franchise agreement is a contractual obligation.

Now this article is not meant to scare the pants off of you or deter you from chasing your dream - but it is meant to point out the "No Bull!" side of getting into a franchise. As I have said before, buying a franchise is serious business and needs to be treated that way. So remember this... a franchise is like getting married, easy to get into, but will be tough and expensive if things go wrong.

If you are serious about buying a franchise and submit the proper paperwork to your prospective franchisor; they will provide you with a document called the Franchise Disclosure Document, or FDD as it is typically referred to. I have seen many a strong man run for their lives when they see this document - it is usually quite thick and comprises of hundreds of pages. But <u>don't be alarmed</u>, it is actually a series of documents assembled together. When it is broken down into pieces, it starts to make more sense and easier to understand. An FDD typically consists of the following documents depending on the concept:

- The FDD itself
- State Regulators and Agents exhibit
- Audited Company Financials (3 years worth)
- Franchise Agreement

- Development Agreement (if offered)
- List of Franchised Locations
- Specific State Addendums
- Personal Guaranty
- Non-Compete and Confidentiality Agreement
- FDD Receipt
- Loan or Finance Documents (if offered)
- Other Franchise Operations specific documents such as Point of Sale, Etc.

Once a franchisor gives you (discloses) their FDD, they will require you to sign a receipt stating that you have received it. By signing, you are under no obligation whatsoever. Franchising is regulated by the Federal Trade Commission (FTC) and the receipt is proof that you were given the FDD at least 14 days prior to paying them a franchise fee or signing any agreements. The 14 day period is required to ensure that a prospective buyer understands the contractual obligations they are entering into.

In addition - the FDD is a wealth of information for you to understand the franchise and company you are evaluating. The FDD contains 23 different items about the franchise including:

- The franchisor's background including the business description in detail.
- The business experience of the principal officers & staff, including bankruptcies & litigation.
- All fees involved with the franchise, including estimated startup costs & terms.
- Technology, trademark, & quality controls.
- Patents & copyrights.
- Training requirements & territory guidelines.
- Renewal, transfer, and dispute resolution.
- Financial Performance Representations (if offered)
- Financing & complete list of all franchisees.

Authors Note: *For more in-depth information on FDD's and what they contain, download a free document "The Federal Trade Commission's Guide to Buying a Franchise" at our website: www.HelgersonFranchiseGroup.com*

So why can't you just quit - you ask.

When you sign your franchise agreement, you have legally obligated yourself to the terms of the franchise agreement; whatever they may be. For example, if the term or duration of the franchise is for ten years, it means that you and your franchisor have agreed, as long as you are in good standing and paid your royalties, etc, you may operate under the terms of your franchise agreement for up to ten years whatever those obligations may be. In addition, most franchises have renewal opportunities for additional terms if you are in good standing.

At the end of the day - if the prospective franchise you are considering has a ten year term, be ready to run a business for the next ten years or longer.

Keep in mind that every year - hundreds, if not thousands of entrepreneurs embark on a new adventure called franchising. Legal documents are a part of business and their objective is to outline the relationship of the parties and what happens if things do not work out. Keep it in perspective and do not let it get in the way of pursuing your dream of owning your own business.

If you live up to your obligations of your franchise agreement like you expect your franchisor to, you will have a long and mutually respective relationship with them.

As Donald Trump would say *"Nothing personal - just business!"*

Don't just hire any lawyer - hire a franchise lawyer.

If there is anything at all that you take away from this handbook, let it be this. Before you sign any agreements with your new franchisor, be sure you absolutely understand your obligations. If needed have an attorney review the franchise agreement.

Here's a big money saving tip!! Hire a *reputable franchise lawyer* that knows and understands these types of agreements. If you hire a standard business lawyer - you will end up paying them to learn the ins and outs of franchising and the agreement. Hiring a good franchise lawyer will make all the difference in the world in evaluating a franchise agreement. They have usually read hundreds of agreements and stay abreast of new changes to franchise law.

Success Tips:

- Be prepared that entering into a franchise is a long term commitment – be ready to work it for the next 10 years or longer.
- Keep the franchise agreement in perspective – *"Nothing personal, just business!"*
- Hire a seasoned *franchise lawyer* if needed.
- Download "The Federal Trade Commission's Guide to Buying a Franchise" at www.HelgersonFranchiseGroup.com

Chapter 4

Not being financially prepared for the investment

Franchising Facts:

- Buying a franchise will require a cash investment at some level.
- 401(k) and home equity are the easiest and quickest financing options.
- Franchisor loans are just like bank loans and must be paid back.

Buying a franchise will require a cash investment at some level.

OK – let's get this out of the way... If you are serious about buying a franchise of some type, as a <u>minimum financial criteria</u> you will need to have at least $20,000 or more in liquid capital (cash, savings/checking, 401(k), thrift savings plans, stocks/bonds) and a net worth of $100,000 or more (Assets - Liabilities = Net Worth) in today's market.

While there may be some franchise opportunities that have lower investment criteria – most will require this level of investment or much more. All franchises have minimum investment criteria you must meet to be eligible to become a franchisee. If you do not meet their minimum criteria, your application will be rejected. Starting a business takes money. And the more of it you have available, the more and different franchise opportunities you will qualify for.

My straight advice to you - if you do not meet this minimum financial requirement, you are best to retain your job and save up cash and savings until you do.

401(k) and home equity is the easiest and fastest finance options.

The recent economic disaster that our country had, and still continues to deal with has had a significant impact on franchise lending. While business loans are still attainable – the time and requirements to complete them have gotten longer and more complex, even for the smallest of loans.

Because of that, one of the fastest growing finance tools is the conversion of 401(k) or other retirement funds into a business investment. You can do this without incurring taxes, penalties, interest or debt. The benefits are powerful with the ability to:

- Invest your retirement funds in your business — without taxes or penalties.
- Use a safe, proven plan based on long standing provisions of the Internal Revenue Service.
- Use pre-tax dollars to fund your business.
- Gain business equity and an improved cash flow position from the start.
- Use the funds to receive a salary during startup.
- Accelerate business profitability by eliminating or reducing interest and debt.
- Secure funding fast—typically two to three weeks or less.
- Set aside tax deductible retirement savings up to $200,000 per year.
- Optimize business equity and value.

Another low-pain financing option is tapping into the equity on your home. You may already have a credit line that your bank has extended to you - or if you need to apply for a home equity line of credit, the turnaround is typically fairly quick depending on your bank.

Concerning finance options in starting a franchise - be sure to explore them all and consult with a personal finance advisor before getting into anything.

Authors Note: *Visit www.HelgersonFranchiseGroup.com for a list of companies that specialize in 401(k) and Thrift Savings Plan finance programs.*

You will have to pay your franchisor loans.

In today's financial market place, getting financing for a franchise can be difficult at best. In order to help with this process, some franchisors have started financing various fees involved with their concept. There almost seems to be as many finance options as there are franchise companies. Some of them will finance just the franchise fee - all the way to some of them that will finance the entire development of the franchise. Not all franchisors offer financing, so be sure to investigate these opportunities when looking at their concept. Keep in mind though - if a franchise does not offer financing you shouldn't think negatively of them. It just means they choose not to be in the banking business.

So does this mean they are giving you free money? Absolutely not! Just as in the Franchise Agreement, you can expect your franchisor to have a sophisticated finance program in place, just like a bank. The franchisor loan documents are just as enforceable as any loan or agreement that you would sign for your home or other conventional business financing.

A good thing to keep in mind... build your credit and your business with your franchisor in a positive way - they will be more apt to want to help you again when it comes to business expansion time.

Success Tips:

- Starting a business takes cold hard cash – be ready for that.
- Use your credit cards sparingly.
- 401(k) and home equity loans can be a quick and easy business loan.
- Explore all financing opportunities with franchisors.
- Remember… at the end of the day - you have to pay all of your debts back, including your franchisor.

Chapter 5

Working in the business – Not on it

Franchising Facts:

- Owning a business will give you more time for yourself - working in it will not.
- It is possible to work yourself out of the business.

Owning a business will give you more time for yourself - working in it will not.

There is nothing I have worked harder at in my life than my business. My marriage to my beautiful bride has been easier and took less time to come to terms with. I hear it time and time again from franchisees old and new that they spend all of their waking moments either thinking or working on their business.

So why would I make such a statement like this? Because... *the business will give you more time to do the things you want to do - if done properly*. Doing it *properly* is the hard part, because this is one segment of business ownership that no one in the world can help you at, except yourself. And as humans, we are our own worst enemies.

Most of us get into a business that we are comfortable with or really enjoy doing. For example, a person that has done janitorial work all their life may feel the best fit for them is a janitorial franchise. That may be true - but this is where the transition from a worker/technician to a business owner becomes a challenge. In reality, most people never make that transition because they get stuck as a worker in their own business. They are stuck because they *love to do the work.* When you are busy working, you never have time to make plans for the future of your business. You have vision capability because you saw the future of yourself owning a business right? Don't let your vision stop after you begin the business - keep your mind on the future and your goals.

Building a business takes proper planning and execution. Most new franchise owners leave their initial training school with a business plan for growing their enterprise. Can you guess where many of them end up? Gathering dust in a desk drawer or on a shelf stuck inside the operations manual that the franchisor loaned them. Why does this happen? Well most of the time it is because on day one, we start answering the phones, helping customers and *working* in our franchise. And then every day, we report to work, over and over again.

So how do you fix this? Well for starters, you need to stick to the plan that you develop in training school. As well, you need a vision of where you want to be in two, five, ten years and beyond. As this vision unfolds, you build an infrastructure sheet for all of the employees that you will need, a pro forma for the business numbers and a formal marketing plan. Then starting day one, you hire job specific employees to handle the work for you, while you then concentrate on managing and growing your business. Each month you compare yourself to where you should be in your plan and make adjustments if needed. Sounds easy right?

Well it is not easy - but it is easier than *working* in your business for eternity. You can have more freedom to do the things you want if you properly plan and execute on it.

It is possible to work yourself out of the business.

Robert T. Kiyosaki, author of the best-selling book *Rich Dad, Poor Dad* said it the best... *"A real business asset does not require my presence. I own them, but they are managed or run by other people. If I have to work there, it's not a business. It becomes my job!"*

To ultimately succeed in business you must devise a plan that ultimately works you out of a job. For example, if you were to purchase and run a janitorial franchise - a simple infrastructure plan might call for janitorial techs, a marketing person, accountant and a manager. When you first begin the business, you hire janitorial techs and all of the other job functions you do yourself. As your business grows, replace yourself with employees that are better at the job function than you. All of a sudden you will realize that you are running an organization that does not depend upon your every waking minute to make money and survive. As you continue your growth you may ultimately have someone running the entire company - allowing you to spend more time on your new boat. Sound great? It can be - but first you must plan and execute.

Remember, you cannot work *on* the business if you are working *in* the business!

Success Tips:

- Franchise systems want business builders – not business workers.
- When buying a franchise, prepare to work yourself out of your business by creating proper business plans.
- Continually focus on working *"on"* the business, not *"in"* the business.

Chapter 6

Going it alone

Franchising Facts:

- Everyone becomes a business expert when asked.
- If your spouse or partner do not approve - franchising is NOT for you!!

Everyone becomes a business expert when asked.

This is a scenario that I have seen many times in my years of franchising. Usually it happens during the discovery phase of franchise shopping with a prospective franchisee and it typically goes something like this...

I was talking to my friend Bob the other day and he told me *"Why don't you just search the internet, buy the equipment yourself and start cleaning for customers. You don't need a franchise company to do this!!"* Since then, I have been asking myself the same question.

The first thing I always ask my candidate is - *"So does Bob own a business?"* I can honestly say in all my years of franchising, no one has ever told me that their friend owns one. But, let's take it one step further and assume he has owned one. So, the next question will be - *"Has Bob ever worked in this type of business before?"* Again, the usual answer is no. So if Bob has never owned or worked in this type of business, what qualifies him to make such a statement?

For starters, we are not beating up on Bob as I am sure he is a great guy and only looking out for his friend's best interest. But in your evaluation of a franchise, you must start thinking like a business person and ask yourself these types of questions. Quickly you will deduct that Bob has no supporting facts to quantify his statement other than he knows you are paying someone a lot of money. As well, Bob has no knowledge of what it takes to build a business or any of the other things it takes to support one. Based upon this analysis you can quickly rule out Bobs comments and continue on with your franchise discovery.

But when you do hear these comments from friends or colleagues, weigh them based upon their direct knowledge and experience. If you want to really get things going - ask them to quantify their statement... But after reading this, you already know what they are probably going to say. Maybe have Bob help you in evaluating franchises - he may find it so interesting you might end up with a partner.

If your spouse or partner do not approve - franchising is NOT for you!!

OK, pay attention on this one... it is short and sweet.

If your spouse or partner does not support you in your business endeavors no matter what they are; it could cost you your marriage or relationship.

I have seen good people end up in tragic circumstances because of this. And believe me; it is more expensive than the cost of your franchise. Your spouse or partner must be 110% behind you as you go forward in your new business.

If you do not have their full support it will not work, end of story, nothing further!

Success Tips:

- Evaluate friends comments about you starting a business based upon their experiences.
- No spouse or partner support = no business!!

Chapter 7

Sticking to what you know

Franchising Facts:

- A franchise can change your career path.
- Continuing education is money well spent.

A franchise can change your career path.

Have you ever heard the line… "The butcher, the baker and the candlestick maker"

That was a long, long time ago when that rhyme was written. Instead of rub a dub, dub, three men in a tub - today the rhyme may only have one man in the tub and he is a multi-unit owner of an M&M Meat Shops® franchise, a Panera Bread® franchise and a Candleman® franchise.

Franchising has come a long way since Cyrus McCormick issued licenses to sell his thrashing machinery all across the country. Today we have what is referred to as *"Business Format"* franchising; whereas all aspects of the franchise are duplicated and trained to franchisees, including customer sales, marketing, operations, accounting functions, and all other business aspects.

So does this mean you can change careers? Absolutely! Most franchise training programs will give you a hands-on, no nonsense approach to their concept. Franchise companies must continually invest into their training programs to ensure that they are staying ahead of the curve and are usually instituting "best practices" gleaned from current operating franchisees.

This type of training is priceless, as you are getting "real world" hands on training.

When evaluating potential franchise concepts remember to ask your franchise representative if they have franchisees that had no prior experience with their type of concept or what type of backgrounds their franchisees had when they joined. Often times you will find people from all walks of life own franchises within any system. However, the best information you can get will come from their current operating franchisees. If you are new to their type of operation; ask their franchisees what background they came from, if the franchisor met their expectations in the training curriculum and if they felt they were adequately prepared to operate their franchise. This will give you a clear picture if the franchise concept is right for you to make a career switch.

Continuing education is money well spent.

Do not let your training end at the initial training session! Just about every franchise system has on-going training programs and annual conventions. Some of the best training I have ever seen - happens at the annual conventions. This is not only a time to acquire additional training, but also a time to make new friends and discover the secrets of high producing franchisees in your system. These high producers have taken what the franchise has provided and built upon it to achieve greater levels. Be sure to sit next to them at all the conferences - because they are always willing to share their success secrets.

The best money you can invest in your franchise business is attending your franchisor conventions and conferences. The benefits of attending greatly outweigh the costs of doing so.

Another great on-going education resource is your local colleges and universities. As you continue to build your franchise, you will require business skill sets that you may not possess. Advanced courses from your local higher education institutions can make all the difference in the world in building your business.

Finally, be sure to join the International Franchise Association (IFA) as a franchisee member. The IFA has the best franchise education programs available today. From attending the annual IFA convention to on-line courses, it is all available to help you succeed in your franchised business.

Success Tips:

- What you're good at doing, may not be the best franchise for you.
- If you want to change careers; interview your potential franchisor and their franchisees *thoroughly* to ensure that they can help you make the transition.
- Never stop your on-going training; it is one of the secrets to business success!
- Make the high performance franchisees in the system your best friends.

Chapter 8

Having lone wolf syndrome

Franchising Facts:

- The essence of franchising is brand consistency.
- You *must* be able to work within a system.

The essence of franchising is brand consistency.

Over the years of interviewing potential franchisees; this topic has came up many times. And each time it does - I must ask the same question...

"If you want to change everything, why are you even looking at buying a franchise?"

I actually lost a potential franchisee once because he wanted to change the color of our brand logo from red to blue. He felt his customers would better relate to a blue logo for some reason. Of course, we did not subdue to his request even though at the time we really needed the cash to grow our fledgling franchise company. The reason we turned him down is because next to franchisees, the brand is the most important asset that a franchise company has. In order to preserve that asset and ensure that the delivery of product or service is uniform a franchise system must have trademark and identity standards that are implemented and *enforced* when necessary.

Occasionally a franchisor will allow slight variations or modifications on specific items, but it will be a very rare occurrence. An example of this may be for specific city zoning requirements or other external influence factors involving outdoor signs, etc. A franchise chain that has this down to a science is McDonald's®. Every one of them is operationally identical and delivers the product with consistency. Although, McDonald's® has aggressive standards that you must adhere to, in certain instances they have allowed franchise owners flexibility in the interior décor of the building. Typically that allowance is for franchisees to decorate in a motif that reflects local geography. Franchisors might allow subtle changes here and there, but do not expect them to budge on certain items such as logo, slogans and other brand specific items.

Remember, the very essence of franchising is consistency and uniformity of their brand, so it is best to accept this policy or move on to something different.

You must be able to work within a system.

This is important, so listen up. If you do not play well with others - franchising is definitely NOT for you.

Franchising depends upon teamwork between the franchisor and the franchisee and between all the franchisees in the system. Does this mean that you are not entitled to your opinion? Of course not, but it does mean that you must get along well with others and be able to work with what the franchisors brand provides you.

Individuals that are strong minded and extremely *entrepreneurial* may have difficulty working within the *confines* of a uniform franchised system. Before jumping into a franchise evaluate yourself carefully in this area.

If you feel that you can take something "prepackaged" and build upon it in a positive way, then you are ready for franchising and franchising is ready for you.

Success Tips:

- Embrace your new franchise brand and follow their standards to the core.
- Be ready to work in a team atmosphere.

Chapter 9

Not sharing your information

Franchising Facts:

- A franchisor needs to know just as much about you as you need to know about them.
- Franchising is a relationship business.
- Being prepared will make you rise above the crowd.

A franchisor needs to know just as much about you as you need to know about them.

A little known secret that prospective franchisees don't realize is that a franchisor pays attention on how you respond to information requests. They use that information in determining whether you are a good fit for their brand and if you should be awarded a franchise or not. At any time in this process you drag your feet or hesitate on sending your information - you are sending them a message on how you might interact with future customers and franchise support staff.

This may sound strange, but it is absolutely true. Traits demonstrated by a prospective franchisee during the discovery and franchise recruiting process typically reflect on how they might run their business. If you are the personality type that puts things off until it becomes a fire and then deals with it, that trait will more often than not show up in the franchise discovery process. Every time you come in contact with your franchisor they are evaluating you for certain criteria. You may even have questions asked of you by their staff that may seem out of place or odd, but those questions are carefully orchestrated to help them better understand your personality traits.

So why does a franchisor need to know all of this about you?

"Because it is their brand name lit up in the sign on the front of the building and they want to ensure it will be well represented!"

They need to learn as much as they can about you to ensure that you are a good fit and ambassador for the brand. Your franchise application can be turned down for a variety of reasons including your financial strength or credit rating. However, a *"great"* franchisor will turn you down if they feel you are not a good "fit" for their system.

The best thing you can do if you are serious about buying a franchise is to respond to the sales staff promptly with the information they need. Believe me - your file will very quickly float to the top of the pile if you do this. Remember, your franchise representative is your champion and will sell you to their superiors if you sell yourself to them.

So be courteous, professional and prompt and do not get annoyed when they ask you for more information. Trust me; you haven't seen anything yet until you are actually dealing with customers in your business.

Franchising is a relationship business.

And it starts in the discovery process. Depending upon the length of your franchise agreement, you will have a long period of time that you will need to get along with your new franchisor. The better you get along with them - the better they will get along with you. If not, the next ten years or whatever your franchise agreement term is could be the longest period of your life. In addition to the contractual obligations that are exercised between both parties; there is an unseen, unsigned relationship agreement. And it expects all parties to get along in a positive professional business like way.

Franchising can change your life in more ways than you can ever imagine. You will make friends with other franchisees and executives from the company that will last a lifetime. Embrace your new franchise system like family and it will embrace you. Not only will they be there to celebrate your success, but they will be there in time of grief or tragedy as well.

Being prepared will make you rise above the crowd.

So you want to look like a super star to your potential new franchisor? Here's how:

Prepare and have ready the following documents. No need to spend a lot of money having them professionally done, but they need to be typed up and neat.

- A cover letter addressed to the CEO of the company explaining why you would be a good fit for their franchise.
- Resume or Biography detailing your background.
- Personal Financial Statement.
- Business Financial Statement and three years tax returns if applicable.
- Any other supporting documentation such as your DD-214 if you are an armed forces veteran. (many franchises offer discounts to veterans)

After you start dialogue with your franchise representative - send all of this information to them immediately. It will put you light years ahead in the process and demonstrate to them that you are the one they should award a franchise to.

Success Tips:

- Be prepared to share personal information.
- Be courteous, prompt and businesslike with your franchise representative.
- Embrace your new franchise like family.
- Have your paperwork ready to go and look and act like a super star.

Chapter 10

Expecting automatic success

Franchising Facts:

- Franchisor supplies the concept, you supply the business.
- Take responsibility for your own business.

Franchisor supplies the concept, you supply the business.

If you think that buying a franchise will give you instant fame and fortune or drive thousands of immediate customers to your business; you have been misinformed. Here it is, straight-forward:

Your franchisor supplies you the brand, tools, training and support to launch a "new" business in your marketplace. Your job is to generate, nurture and retain customers for the "new" business in your marketplace.

But wait a minute, you thought... THEY were going to supply you with customers?! This is a classic mistake that some people make when they purchase their franchise and then later discover that the reason they are struggling is *their* fault. Quite simply they did not do their homework prior to jumping into the deal or do anything to build the business afterwards. In rare cases, can you open a new franchise location and have customers rush into it. The reality is that you must advertise and market for those customers to come to your location.

Doing adequate due diligence prior to purchasing your franchise will give you good information on what it will take to *build* your business. Find out who the highest producers are in the system, ask them what it took to build their business, and be prepared to work at it.

Take responsibility for your own business.

This is something that is almost ubiquitous amongst struggling franchise owners. They have not taken responsibility for their business. Let's take a closer look... whose name is on the corporation or partnership? Whose name is on the federal and state tax returns? Whose name is on the sales tax license? Whose name is on the business permit? Whose name is on the business loan? And on and on - you get the picture.

You will be the CEO of your new business and you must take full responsibility for its failures as well as its success. People quickly accept responsibility for success but will tend to find reason for failure outside of them. It is a human defense trait, we can't help it. But it has no place in business. Not taking responsibility for your business doesn't mean you will go to jail for it, unless of course you do something illegal. But it might mean that you could lose your investment and that is something you do not want to do. Your franchisor is always willing to help you in building your business. Do not let your pride get in the way of taking their business advice and acting on it. Remember, they want to see you as successful as you can be.

No question - building a successful business takes a lot of hard work. But it also takes a strong leader that is ready to accept the responsibility - good or bad.

Are you that leader? Are you ready for franchising?

Success Tips:

- Complete your due diligence and model yourself after the high producers of the franchise system.
- Be prepared to take responsibility for your business - good or bad.

Chapter 11

Bonus section for veterans

Franchising Facts:

- Franchisors want more veterans in their franchise systems.
- Franchise fee discounts and/or special financing by franchisors are available for veterans.
- Veteran business loan options.

Franchisors want more veterans in their franchise systems.

The late Don Dwyer Sr., founder of The Dwyer Group, founded VetFran as a way to say thank you to our veterans returning from the first Gulf war. His daughter Dina Dwyer-Owens, the past Chairwoman of the International Franchise Association (IFA), re-energized the program after the Sept. 11, 2001 terrorist attacks.

As a component of the IFA, VetFran's ranks have grown to include hundreds of franchise systems that voluntarily offer financial discounts and financial incentives to veterans seeking to become franchise owners. Since the inception of VetFran – more than 2,500 veterans have followed their dream of small business ownership through franchising.

Veterans and franchising is a great match for many reasons including:

- Demonstrated leadership qualities.

- Know how to follow and work within a documented system.
- Ask for help when needed.
- Veterans persevere.
- Know how to build and manage teams.
- Have a "get it done" attitude.
- They have dedication to the mission.

Franchise fee discounts and/or special financing are available for veterans.

As a program of the IFA, all franchise companies that participate in VetFran are required to offer some special incentive to veterans. That incentive must be in the form of discounted franchise fees or other types of special financing. In addition to the IFA's VetFran program efforts - other non IFA member companies have started promoting veteran incentive programs.

Veteran business loan options.

Unfortunately at this time our government does very little to support veterans looking to get into a business. Grants and other "free business money" from the Veterans Administration (VA) or other government agencies are an urban myth and simply do not exist. Possibly there might be some types of small grants or loan programs at the state or private level - but none that I have personally heard about or found.

In light of that, there are a couple of options available. The first one is the Small Business Administration (SBA) Patriot Express Loan. To take advantage of this program, a veteran needs to create a relationship with a regional bank or other lending institution that provides and facilitates SBA loans. I highly recommend working with an SBA preferred lender, as preferred lenders can streamline the process and typically get a loan done quicker.

The process for the Patriot Express Loan is much the same as any other SBA loan program, so be prepared to provide the necessary documentation, have adequate investment capital, loan collateralization, and creditworthiness.

Another option, and in my opinion, the quickest and easiest, is utilizing government Thrift Saving Plans (TSP) to fund a new business. Much like a 401(k) rollover, these programs can convert qualified retirement plans in a tax free manner into a franchise business investment. The caveat for these rollovers is that you must be separated from service to be eligible for this type of transaction. For more information on 401(k) and TSP rollover programs please refer back to Chapter 4.

Success Tips:

- Visit the VetFran program at www.franchise.org for more information.
- Explore all veteran financing options when researching companies.
- Work with veteran assistance programs such as Veteran Franchise Centers at www.VeteranFranchiseCenters.com

Index

About the Author

Lonnie Helgerson, CFE

Serial Frantrepreneur, Noted Franchise Expert, Author, Speaker, and Bad Golfer.

With over 26 years in the franchise industry working with companies such as Super 8 Motels and Ident-A-Kid. He is recognized as the pioneer in the mobile computer service franchise sector as the founder of Computer Doctor - the first franchise of its kind and two other franchise chains; Expetec Technology Services & InstantFX Web Services.

Currently he is Co-Founder & President of both Veteran Franchise Centers, a franchise brand that provides free matching services to veterans entering into franchise opportunities and Helgerson Franchise Group.

He is a frequent speaker and facilitator for the International Franchise Association, Franchisor Association of Florida and many other various franchise and business seminars.

Additionally, he serves as the Immediate Past Chairman of the VetFran committee of the International Franchise Association, IFA Franchisor Forum, the Institute of Certified Franchise Executives Board of Governors, the Board of Advisor's of The International Institute of Franchise Education, H. Wayne Huizenga School of Business and Entrepreneurship in Ft. Lauderdale, FL, and the Franchisor Association of Florida Board of Directors.